HOW WE USED TO LIVE
1954 · 1970

FREDA KELSALL

A & C Black in association with **Yorkshire Television**

Acknowledgements

Historical advisor, Norman Longmate.

Pictures by Barnaby's Picture Library pages 17 (centre), 25 (bottom), 32 (top), 33 (bottom); Copyright BBC (Enterprises) page 26 (top); BBC Hulton Picture Library pages 18 (top), 23 (top), 38 (top); Clive Coreless from the Conran Directory of Design page 5 (bottom left); Cranks Wholefoods page 27 (bottom); reproduced by permission of the Daily Express page 14 (bottom); Daily Telegraph Colour Library page 32 (bottom left); Mike Hardy/Daily Telegraph Colour Library 33 (top); John Frost Newspapers pages 34, 35; Henry Grant pages 5 (bottom right), 13 (right top and bottom), 22 (bottom); H. J. Heinz Company Ltd. page 20 (top); photo Don McCullin/Sunday Times, London page 36 (top); National Film Archive London pages 18 (bottom), 39 (bottom right); Oxfam page 39 (top); The Photo Source pages 3, 7 (bottom), 11 (left), 14 (top), 22 (top), 29 (bottom), 30 (bottom), 40 (centre), 47; Polaroid Corporation page 41 (bottom); Popperfoto pages 4 (left), 5 (top left), 6 (top), 8, 10, 11 (top right), 16 (top), 18 (centre), 24, 26 (bottom), 28 (top), 30 (top), 31 (bottom right), 32 (bottom right), 33 (centre), 36 (bottom left and right), 37 (bottom left), 40 (top), 41 (top), 42 (top, centre), 46; Quadrant/Autocar page 17 (top); David Redfern/DRP page 29 (centre); Rex Features page 37 (top left); RoSPA page 17 (bottom); Sainsbury's page 27 (top); W. H. Smith & Son Ltd. page 28 (bottom); Time Out page 39 (left); Topham pages 5 (top right), 6 (bottom), 7 (top), 9 (top), 11 (bottom right), 12, 15, 19 (top, bottom, centre right), 21 (centre, bottom), 23 (bottom), 29 (top), 31 (bottom left, top), 37 (right), 38 (bottom), 42 (bottom), 44, 45; Town and Country Planning Association page 9 (bottom); N. Wright/National Motor Museum page 16 (bottom); Polydor International GmbH, Hamburg page 43 (top); reproduced by permission of Penguin Books Ltd. pages 13 (top left) (copyright © Leila Berg 1948, 1966; illustrations copyright © Edward Standon, 1966), 20 (bottom) (Puffin Books 1968); page 25 (top) © Yorkshire Television Ltd.

How We Used to Live is a Yorkshire Television production. Executive producer, Chris Jelley; Producers, Ian Fell, Carol Wilks.

Front cover photograph shows singers Billy Fury and Vince Eager in Yarmouth © Popperfoto
Back cover photograph shows the Brady family from the Yorkshire Television series 'How We Used to Live (1954–1970)' © Yorkshire Television Ltd.

Contents

British Library Cataloguing in Publication Data

Kelsall, Freda
    How we used to live, 1954–1970.
    1. Great Britain   Social life and customs
        1945–
    I. Title
    941.085'5   DA589.4

    ISBN 0-7136-2925-8

Published by A & C Black (Publishers) Limited
35 Bedford Row, London WC1R 4JH

First published 1987
Text copyright © 1987 by Freda Kelsall

Typeset by Method Ltd, Epping, Essex
Printed by Resopal Lda, Portugal

A time of change

'Everything's taking a turn for the better, mark my words!'
Auntie Bertha in 1954, from the Yorkshire Television series 'How We Used to Live (1954–70)'.

The period that spanned 1954–1970 was a time of rapid change, which affected the way people dressed, the food they ate, their jobs and their spare time. For the first time young people had money and influence. Teenagers were determined to 'do their own thing' and they demanded that adults should take notice of them.

In 1954 there were still bomb sites in some cities, grim reminders of the Second World War. Some food was still rationed. But the mood was changing. People were fed up with austerity, and the way they enjoyed the Festival of Britain in 1951, and the Coronation of Queen Elizabeth in 1953 was a sign that people felt optimistic and keen to try anything that was new, colourful and above all, young.

Fly me to the moon was a fifties pop song which nobody took seriously. Who could have predicted that just over a decade later, a man really would walk on the moon? Or that pop music would have changed beyond all recognition?

Above all people felt that things were getting better, that Britain was moving towards a society less divided by class, and new technology would mean that there were plenty of new opportunities to grasp: 'My strongest memory is of being a youth when youth had a say' … 'These were amazingly exciting times. There was an opening-up of the world to ordinary people.' (*John, aged 15 in 1961*)

At home

'We had Festival of Britain wallpaper – on one wall only!'
Jessica, aged 10 in 1954

In the fifties the word for anything new and smart was 'contemporary'. Many families learned about modern design at the Festival of Britain exhibition, which was held in London in 1951, and wanted to try the new styles in their own homes.

A 'contemporary' kitchen might be covered in red and grey formica, and have new time-saving gadgets like an electric toaster and kettle. Families began to replace their austere war-time furniture with goods made of new practical plastic and polythene. Fifties design made rooms look light and spacious, with easy-to-clean surfaces. One woman remembers 'We had plastic curtains in the kitchen, with a design of French pavement cafés.'

Although some families owned new labour-saving machines, many homes in the fifties were cleaned with mops and carpet sweepers. A decade later, most families had a vacuum cleaner, as well as a telephone, refrigerator, and television.

Dust traps, like picture rails and iron fireplaces, were covered up or removed to make rooms easier to clean and less cluttered. When central heating became more easily available, many people decided to get rid of their coal fires, especially as the Clean Air Act, which became law in 1956, banned smoky chimneys in cities.

▲ This 1956 hallway has geometric floor-tiles, cocktail-cherry coat pegs and contrasting wall papers. Indoor plants were popular fifties decor.

◄ A fitted kitchen in 1965. Easy-to-clean, matching units replaced old wooden cupboards.

▲ Many people bought new time-saving gadgets which became widely available in the fifties.

▲ A 1970 open-plan dining area, with fashionable chrome, smoked glass and muted colours. More people now had the sort of lifestyle that previously only the rich could afford.

In the living room, fashionable fifties furniture had spindly legs and sophisticated abstract design. The Festival of Britain and fifties abstract art inspired the contrasting geometric designs of wallpaper and carpets. It was fashionable to cover one wall in one design and the other three in another, and to create an impression of space and light.

In the mid-sixties metal tubes and uncluttered Scandinavian furniture made of perspex gave rooms a futuristic look. One fad was paper chairs, a throw-away fashion, typical of the period. Bold swirly patterns were popular, in sharp black-and-white or vivid psychedelic colours like orange, purple and raspberry pink. By 1967, the Eastern influence of the hippies showed in many young people's rooms – even if it was just one Indian rug draped on the wall.

At the end of the sixties there was another complete change in style for the home. Instead of looking for brand-new homes and furniture, young couples chose to buy converted Victorian houses, and searched in junk shops for furniture to match. For the first time, second-hand became chic. Plastic and chrome were out, now everyone wanted to buy pine furniture and decorate their homes in styles very like those of the early years of the century. Even fashionable colours were darker – olive-green and sludge.

▲ This boldly spotted sixties paper chair was not meant to last a lifetime, and the plastic chair was designed for its dramatic appearance rather than for comfort.

Changing landscapes

'I had a love of all skyscrapers, the taller the better. I never thought what it would be like to live in one.'
John, aged 14 in 1960.

After the war, there was a shortage of homes. Many families were living in overcrowded, unsafe buildings. In the early fifties, a woman noticed that 'From the train into Waterloo you could see miles of terraced slums'. By the end of the sixties they had vanished. Between 1950 and 1970 over a million homes were demolished in slum clearance.

▲ Most towns grow from villages. Harlow New Town was planned and built as a whole on empty green field sites as one way to solve the housing shortage.

The Government, local councils and private builders tackled the job of providing new places for people to live. One plan was to move hundreds of people out of the cities into new towns built on green fields in the country. Jobs, shops, schools, everything anyone needed, were all close at hand. However, it didn't take long for residents to discover that New Towns had real disadvantages. Young couples who were used to living just around the corner from their families, felt a very long way from them.

◄ Old houses were demolished in spite of the protests of residents. Thousands of people were rehoused in tower blocks.

In cities, not all the new homes were built at ground level. Tower blocks seemed a good idea; building upwards seemed a way of providing many more homes without using up much expensive land. At first, people were pleased with their 'high-rise' flats. 'I really liked the view from the eighth floor', one woman said when she moved into her new flat in 1962. But opinions about tower blocks soon changed. Young mothers felt marooned in the towers, a frighteningly long way from where their children played below. People found it hard to make friends or talk to their new neighbours. One teenager thought it was 'Horrifying. I was sick over the balcony of one in Sowerby Bridge'.

By the end of the sixties, people looked at the old terraced houses in a different way. They were no longer slums to be knocked down. With a home improvement grant from the council to pay for a new roof, an indoor toilet, safe electric wiring, replacing rotten wood, and a cure for the damp, these houses could be made into homes where families could live comfortably.

▲ Ronan point. In 1968 a gas explosion in this tower block killed three people, adding to widespread criticism of these buildings.

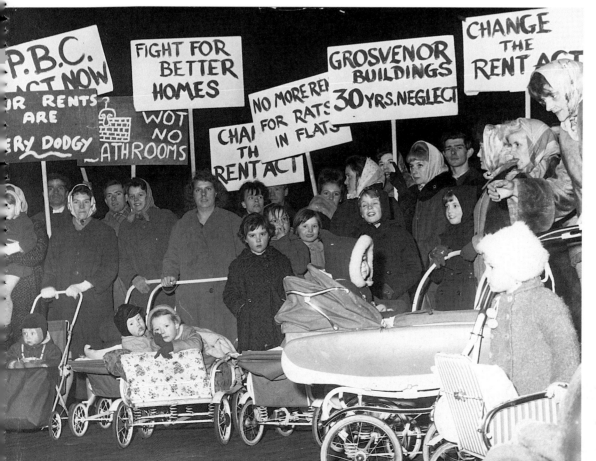

◄ Some landlords took advantage of the housing shortage by charging high rents, often for overcrowded squalid flats. For many people this was the only alternative to being homeless.

7

▼ In 1953, flags for the Coronation were mass-produced on simple treadle sewing machines.

▶ Car-sprayers working on an assembly line in 1963. Automation speeded up production but made work more boring and reduced the numbers of jobs.

At work

'We changed to aerosol containers, polishes, hair lacquer. Not that there was much to do except mind the conveyer belt. The machines did all the work.'
Robert, a factory worker aged 20 in 1962

Over the period spanning the fifties and sixties, many workplaces became more attractive, both inside and out. As electricity was used more widely, big coal furnaces were no longer needed to fuel the factories, and smoky mill chimneys began to disappear from the landscape. New multi-storey office blocks were built for expanding businesses such as insurance or advertising.

The technology used in offices and factories developed rapidly. Modern factories used more machines and fewer people. However, most workers had a job in the fifties and sixties – Britain was enjoying a consumer boom. There was a huge demand for new products, especially luxuries and plastic goods.

Traditional 'heavy' industries suffered from competition from overseas. Ship-building, and iron and steel works used out-of-date equipment and buildings, and it was cheaper and easier to import from countries like Japan and West Germany. Some workers in these industries found that their skills were no longer needed.

Dockland areas, in particular, changed completely. Dockworkers were no longer needed to unload goods at the docks, pack them into containers and put them onto ships. Instead, container lorries arrived at the docks, prepacked so that the goods could be loaded straight on to the ships. This speeded things up but it cut out hundreds of people's jobs. Workers called 'wild-cat' strikes, when they would down tools without warning to cause as much disruption as they could.

The chemical industry provided many new jobs. There was a huge demand for all sorts of new chemical-based products – including synthetic fabrics like nylon and polyester, artificial fertilisers for farming, and detergents and plastic emulsion paint for the home.

◄ Chickens being packed for freezing. Until the fifties, chicken was an annual Christmas treat. With the introduction of battery farming, freezing and mass-production methods, like the conveyor belt, chicken was no longer a luxury.

Farming became more intensive: instead of working the land, a farmer might be in charge of maintaining an artificially-controlled environment for battery chickens.

On the high street, the rapid spread of chain stores, like Marks & Spencer, meant that the same shops were found in every major town across the country. Supermarkets began to replace small grocers, bakers and butchers. Shoppers found it saved time having a wide range of products under one roof, although, at first, older people were less happy about having to serve themselves.

With so many goods competing on the supermarket shelves, manufacturers had to think of ways to make shoppers buy their particular product. They spent more money on packaging and advertising to attract the customer. This meant more work for marketing executives, commercial artists and photographers.

With so many new opportunities, young people could nearly always find work, and careers teachers simply helped them to choose from all the jobs on offer.

◄ Traffic-free shopping precincts, like this one in Crawley New Town, changed the face of the High Street. Large chain stores were able to charge less than small shops so many people now went shopping once a week at the supermarket, rather than every day at the local shops.

Working conditions

'The Trade Unions? They want jam on it!
We're pensioners, we know all about freeze
and squeeze. But if *we* went on strike, who'd
notice?'
Uncle Albert, from the Yorkshire Television series
'How We Used to Live (1954–1970)'.

During the early fifties, there were few
industrial disputes. In 1955 there was a
long dock strike, followed by a rail strike
which caused so much disruption that the
Government called a state of emergency. Both
these strikes were warnings of what was ahead.

'We don't welcome mass introduction of
machinery just to help the government get half
a million people on the dole,' said a shop
steward in 1956. People wanted a share in the
large profits of their firms. Their Unions tried
to protect them from the effects of rising prices
by bargaining with the management to keep
wages up. The Government and employers
kept wages high enough for many people to
buy the new goods being mass-produced on the
new machinery.

Most families were now able to buy things that
had previously only been luxuries such as
refrigerators and television sets. For a few years
there seemed plenty of money to go round and
lots of things to spend it on.

In the mid-sixties it became more difficult to
sell British products abroad because they were
very expensive compared with the same
products in other countries. The Government
tried to solve this by devaluing the pound so
that foreign goods imported to this country
were far more expensive: the 'pound in your
pocket' would buy the same amount of British
products but French wines, Dutch cheese and
Japanese transistor radios would cost more.

▲ The departure board at Waterloo station showed that
because of a nationwide rail strike there were no trains for
Whitsun holiday-makers in 1955. The government made
emergency plans to distribute food, milk and fuel in case
the strike went on for a long time.

In 1965–66, the Government passed laws to
protect workers' rights. People who were made
redundant were paid money related to the
length of time they had worked for their
company. People who were laid off, or on sick
leave, were to receive benefits related to their
wages when they were still at work, and old age
pensions were increased.

▼ In 1969 the Labour government announced a plan
called 'In Place of Strife' which proposed to strengthen
workers' rights but limit the disruption caused by strikes.
Behind the plan was Barbara Castle, one of the few
women politicians of the time.

Responsible Trade Unionists did a great deal to improve their workers' living standards in the fifties and sixties, even if they needed to strike to make their point. Not all disputes were with the management – sometimes different Unions struggled against each other over who had the right to do certain jobs.

Women at work were not treated as well as men. They were paid less for doing the same jobs and had few prospects of promotion. Until 1970, there was no law on equal pay for doing the same work and, in Parliament, the debate on equal opportunities for women was virtually ignored until the seventies.

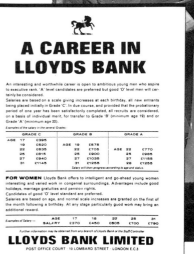

▲ Women were normally paid less for doing the same work as men, and were not expected to be as serious about their careers, as this 1965 advertisement shows.

▲ 1966. The first girl in her college to gain an HNC in building. Gradually, women succeeded in breaking into careers previously reserved for men.

◄ A demonstration by young unemployed men in 1963. By the end of the sixties, unemployment was beginning to become a problem.

▼ In 1961 friendly students welcomed immigrants from the Commonwealth arriving at Waterloo on the boat train.

In the fifties and throughout most of the sixties, there was work for most people. Many of the less popular jobs couldn't be filled, and London Transport invited people from the Caribbean and other areas of the Commonwealth to help staff the Underground and buses, while the National Health Service recruited Asian doctors and nurses. However, many highly qualified black people who emigrated to Britain were met with racial prejudice and found it difficult to get a job to suit their abilities.

Schools

'Dad, why am I borderline?'
'Borderline means you're a good all-rounder.
Nobody can decide the kind of school you're
best suited for.'
*Peter and Jimmy, from the Yorkshire Television
series 'How We Used to Live (1954–1970)'.*

Some of the biggest changes in the fifties and
sixties took place in schools. Until the end of the
sixties, children at primary schools took an
exam called the 11+ in their last year of junior
school. The exam was to select boys and girls
for the local grammar schools, where they
would have to study subjects like Latin and
trigonometry. They would be expected to take
GCE 'O'level and 'A'level exams and to go on
to university or train for a professional career.

The children who weren't selected for a
grammar school went to a secondary modern
school where they would do more practical
subjects like metal-work and domestic science.
Often children left at fifteen without any
qualifications on paper.

Since the war, some excellent secondary
modern schools had opened in bright new
buildings. They were mainly concerned with
turning out good all-rounders, with experience
in practical subjects, although some children
stayed on into the fifth form and passed enough
'O'levels to go on to further education.

But many people were convinced that schools
could be run in a better way. They felt that the
11+ exam was unfair, especially as the pass
mark varied in different areas of the country. A
person's whole future could be decided at
eleven years old, and parents didn't like the
idea of their children being branded as failures.

▼ A purpose-built Essex comprehensive school in 1969.

hou jon caut the see-hors

liela berg

inifhial teechiŋ alfabet edifhon

a yuŋ puffin   5/-

◄ The Initial Teaching Alphabet was invented by Pitman, who also invented shorthand. Each letter represented one sound. It was tried out in the sixties as a way of making learning to read easier.

▲ Traditional ways of learning maths, like doing sums from the blackboard, did not seem enough for the new computer age. These sixties children are using blocks to experiment and develop ideas about numbers.

In 1965, the government told local education authorities to prepare plans for comprehensive schools where children of all abilities could be taught together. By 1969 most authorities had done this, although some argued bitterly that it would mean lowering standards, not to mention the muddle while they reorganised themselves.

Primary schools no longer had to push children towards the fearful 11+, so they became less formal and much less competitive. Instead of learning poems off by heart and chanting multiplication tables, there was more project work, more chance to experiment and learn by doing. New ways of teaching were tried out, like the Initial Teaching Alphabet and 'New Maths'.

For young people who were able to stay on at school, there were greater opportunities for further education. More new universities were opened and money was spent on upgrading colleges of higher education.

In 1969, the most ambitious plan of all was under way: the Open University (based in the new town of Milton Keynes) provided degree courses for people to study at home, especially adults who might have missed earlier chances by being labelled 11+ 'failures' as children.

▲ Sussex was one of the universities which opened in the sixties offering a wide range of new degree courses, such as sociology or catering.

Getting around

'I don't know why you keep moaning about the railway closing, Dad. How often have we been on a train since we got the Mini?'
Anthony, from the Yorkshire Television series 'How We Used to Live (1954–70)'.

In just three years, from 1955–58, the number of cars on British roads doubled. Few people had predicted the rapid growth of car ownership – when Harlow New Town was first planned, only one garage was thought to be needed between ten houses. By the end of the fifties it was clear that there would have to be some new solutions to keep all this traffic moving freely and without enormous jams.

In 1959 the first stretch of motorway was opened, the M1 which was to connect London with the North. In the same year, the first bypass was opened, 8½ miles (13½ kms) round Preston. It had cost £3¾ million and had taken more than two years to build. It was clear that building and maintaining Britain's roads was going to take a lot of time and money.

Until 1963, Britain had a 13 000 mile (21 000 km) network of railways. Each rural town and village had its own railway station. In 1963, Dr Beeching led an enquiry which made the Government decide to cut these branch lines to save money.

▲ In 1970 a roundabout and flyover were added to the Westway in London. Many people lost their homes when motorways were built across residential areas, however motorists welcomed these roads which made it much easier to get into and out of major cities.

About half of the stations and a third of all the tracks were closed. It was a good way of saving money, but it meant that many people in the country lost their links with mainline stations. Buses were often infrequent and many people had to buy a car or move house!

Nearly everyone was upset about the Beeching cuts. One man said 'I felt it was a terrible mistake to close useful and friendly branch lines and their flower-bedded stations with the names picked out in whitened stones'.

"Dr. Beeching's plan to streamline the railways don't provide separate freight for Lady Ringboan's 'orse."
Daily Express, March 28th, 1963

▲ Giles, the cartoonist, gave his opinion of the Beeching cuts in the Daily Express, 1963.

As having a car became more important, the city landscape changed. Trolley buses, attached to overhead electric wires had run round London for many years, but in 1962 they disappeared. In the same year trams ran for the last time in the streets of Glasgow.

People were getting more adventurous about foreign travel. In the late fifties, package holidays became more widely available and many people flew for the first time. Gatwick Airport was opened and the latest aircraft, the Boeing 707, came into service. Air travel was no longer just for the wealthy few.

▲ The way that people travelled each day changed in the fiftes and sixties. Buses gradually took over tram and trolley routes and steam trains were replaced by diesel locomotives.

▼ Many enthusiasts formed groups to keep the memory of the old trains alive.

Transport: new ideas

'I had a Vespa in 1959. It was red, one year old, and cost £100, which I paid off over two years. I loved the freedom it gave me. I kept it six years, and sold it, still in good nick, for £10 when I left for Africa'.

Anne, a teenager in 1959.

In the fifties many people had the freedom of being able to own their own transport for the first time. People who were then teenagers remember mopeds with affection, although one woman says that hers 'made a noise like a bumblebee in a cocoa tin'. At the time, crash helmets weren't compulsory, and riders and passengers were sometimes scornful of 'skid-lids'.

When you sold your moped, your next buy might have been a bubble car, a tiny odd-shaped three-wheeler which was hardly big enough for two. One man remembers seeing a girl lifting the rear end of a bubble car to park it more tidily.

But even bubble cars were eclipsed by the popularity of the Mini, which first appeared in showrooms in 1959. It was just big enough to hold a small family, economical with petrol, and at a price that people could afford. It was also easy to park.

In the early fifties there were few parking restrictions and people just left their cars anywhere. By the late fifties, this had become a problem, and the first parking meters and traffic wardens were introduced in the major cities. Meters were an American idea and many people thought they would never catch on in this country because British cars were a wider variety of sizes than American cars.

▲ Mopeds were cheap, easy to run and fun. Young people could be independent, without having to rely on public transport.

▼ The whole of the front of a bubble car opened up for the driver and one passenger to climb in. Bubble cars were fun to drive but vulnerable in accidents.

◀ A student sport in the sixties was cramming as many people as possible into a mini.

▶ One craze of the late sixties was to decorate cars in psychedelic colours and patterns.

As town centres were redeveloped in the sixties, the wasteground left after buildings were demolished was often used as car parks. When this was insufficient, the developers built multi-storey car parks which rose up 'like concrete egg-boxes'.

With so many more cars on the roads, road safety became even more important. Zebra crossings were introduced and, at first, they were not popular with motorists. Lollipop attendants went on duty outside schools to help children cross over busy roads and, on television, a little squirrel called Tufty was used to teach children to look both ways before they crossed the road.

▲ Each child who joined the Tufty Club was given a badge and a book of stories teaching road safety.

17

Television and radio

'I saw a programme about it—*Tonight*. Like a sort of teatime news. You'd enjoy it, Michael, it doesn't pull any punches.'
'I can hear all the news on the wireless.'
'They can't show you maps on the wireless.'
'I wouldn't have a TV as a gift.'
Bertha and Michael, from the Yorkshire Television series 'How We Used to Live (1954–1970)'.

Many people saw TV for the first time when they watched the Coronation in 1953. After that, sales of televisions soared. Cabinets tended to be large and screens small, with pictures only in black and white, but TV quickly became part of family life.

The BBC was very formal at the time. The presenters wore smart evening dress, and all programmes stopped after tea so that children could be put to bed. When a second channel, ITV, opened in 1955 it had a less formal style of broadcasting. ITV was paid for by advertisements between the programmes. Young children picked up jingles, like 'You'll wonder where the yellow went, when you brush your teeth with Pepsodent', as fast as they learned nursery rhymes.

Television affected other forms of entertainment. A family outing to the pictures cost more than renting a TV for a whole week. Cinema newsreels couldn't compete with the TV news in your own living room.

Radio programmes still had a following, though nothing like as large as the previous decade. *The Goon Show* provided a new brand of zany comedy which quickly became a cult. But apart from a few isolated music programmes (such as the *6.5 Special*) there was little on the television or radio for young people in the fifties and early sixties.

▶ The illustrated news magazine, *Picture Post*, had been very successful during the war. However, it could not compete with television and closed down in 1957.

▲ Spike Milligan, Harry Secombe and Peter Sellars were the Goons, on the popular radio comedy shows.

▶ Tony Hancock was a comedian who moved successfully from radio to television. In his shows he made people laugh with his portrayal of a man confused by modern life.

▲ Teenagers welcomed Radio Caroline as a station that played their kind of music. Many disc jockeys, including Tony Blackburn, began their careers on 'Caroline', and later moved to BBC Radio One.

◄ *Private Eye* magazine started in 1961, and became famous for its mockery of important people and events.

In 1964, Radio Caroline started broadcasting non-stop pop music from a ship in the North Sea. This 'pirate' radio was very popular with teenagers, but the government declared it illegal. In 1967 the BBC started Radio 1 which broadcast all-day pop music. The presenters were known as disc jockeys and became the new celebrities.

In the early sixties, comedy shows run by young people found more and more outrageous ways of making viewers laugh. A programme called *That Was The Week That Was* introduced satire to television. Anyone or anything that was thought to be out-of-date became a target for the show. A new magazine, *Private Eye*, also mocked 'the Establishment'. Young people were having more say in the media and even Prime Ministers could no longer rely on automatic respect from the public.

By the late sixties, some TV humour seemed like anarchy to older viewers. *Monty Python's Flying Circus* broke all the traditional rules of comedy – most sketches didn't even have a punch line.

The Archers and other radio serial stories had become part of everyday life. In 1960, television also started a long running series about the lives of a group of families in the industrial north: *Coronation Street* proved that TV plays didn't have to be about rich people in posh drawing rooms to be successful. Even so, one of the most successful sixties dramas, *The Forsythe Saga*, was about a wealthy family at the turn of the century, and when it was broadcast on Sundays it was so popular that some churches changed the time of the evening service rather than lose their congregations.

◄ The first cast of the long-running series *Coronation Street* celebrates Christmas.

YOU KNOW WHAT

BEANZ MEANZ

▲ A sixties poster for Heinz beans. Constant advertising made an 'image' so familiar that the public could recognise instantly which brand was being promoted.

▼ The Puffin Club was started in 1967 when a lot of exciting new books were being published for children. Children could afford to buy paperback Puffin books with their pocket money.

The media and the public

'Colour supplements were a treat to start with, but then I saw they were advertising gimmicks.'
Jo, a young mum in 1962

Television wasn't the only form of media to become more wi̶ ̶̶ad in the fifties and sixties. People had more leisure time for entertainment, and young people in particular were more sophisticated in their tastes. Many newspapers changed their image to sell more copies, and in 1962 the *Sunday Times* became the first newspaper to launch a colour magazine with the main paper.

Your 'image', or what the public could be made to think about you, was a sixties idea which affected almost everything from politicians to frozen peas. People would be stopped in the street and asked how they would vote at an election, which brand of coffee they preferred, or what they had watched on TV recently. It was easy to get confused by the claims made in advertisements, and *Which* magazine was launched by the Consumers' Association to help people choose what to buy.

As television became more popular, library book loans increased – perhaps because viewers were discovering new areas of interest. Book covers became brighter and more books were published for children.

In the 'swinging sixties', subjects which had rarely been mentioned in public began to be discussed openly. A classic book, *Lady Chatterley's Lover*, caused a stir. An attempt was made to ban the book for being too open about sex, but the attempt failed. Censorship was on the way out. Some people felt that changes were being made too quickly and in 1964, Mrs Mary Whitehouse began campaigning to 'Clean Up TV'.

◀ 007 James Bond – a star of the sixties. His exciting adventures chasing spies and beautiful women captured people's imagination.

▼ *Thunderbirds* was a very popular TV programme for sixties children. Each week, the puppets used fantastic technology to solve a new threat to mankind.

A new freedom was also felt in the cinema. Film-makers during the fifties and sixties made some memorable films, from Alfred Hitchcock's *Psycho*, to *The Sound of Music*. James Dean became a teenage hero in *Rebel Without a Cause*.

By the end of the sixties two new advances, colour television and live broadcasting by satellite, were in use. A film of *The Royal Family* on colour TV, showed the everyday life of the Queen and her relatives to a huge public. It seemed a long way from 1953 when it had taken a great deal of persuasion before cameras were allowed inside Westminster Abbey to televise the Coronation.

▶ In 1969 the investiture of the Prince of Wales was broadcast live on television. It was one of the earliest programmes to be shown in colour.

Indoor entertainment

'They've turned our local palais into a bowling alley and fings ain't what they used to be ...'
From a song by Lionel Bart, 1960

In the fifties evening entertainment was aimed more and more at young people. The word 'teenager' was first used in the fifties to describe young people who had money and freedom and were looking for a chance to show that they were different from the older generation. New plays and films were aimed at the younger generation who provided many of the new ideas themselves.

Dance halls were filled with energetic teenagers jiving to rock 'n' roll music played by live bands. Dancing to records only really caught on after the first discotheques, as they were known, opened in London in the early sixties. When they were tired of dancing, teenagers would go in crowds to a late night coffee-bar to drink cups of espresso coffee.

Theatres and music hall variety shows, which were used to offering a different attraction each week, suffered as more people bought televisions. Many closed down and actors tried to find new jobs in television.

▲ 1962 saw a new dance craze – the Twist. The Beatles later reached the top of the charts with *Twist and Shout*.

▼ A London espresso coffee bar in 1955. These bars were packed with young people who would meet to chat and listen to the juke b

▲ By 1968 many old theatres had been converted into bingo halls.

When bingo became legal in 1960, it brought the older generation back to town for a flutter, and many old cinemas and theatres reopened as bingo palaces.

In 1956 the theatre world was jolted by a play from the new generation – John Osborne's *Look Back in Anger*. Until then, plays had had glamorous settings and had been about the upper classes rather than ordinary people. In *Look Back in Anger* the hero's criticism of old ideas excited the audience. There was nothing glamorous about the setting: it was the first of a type of play nicknamed 'kitchen sink' drama which showed the lives of ordinary people.

The sixties mood of freedom and confidence showed in films and plays. Although large theatres were closing, new small independent theatre groups performed in church halls and schools, and on the 'fringe' of West End theatres. Soon there was so much going on that listings magazines were published to tell people what they could go and see.

Until 1968 the Lord Chamberlain officially censored all plays to make sure that nothing in them could shock the audience. When censorship was stopped, an extraordinary new play shocked London and New York: in *Hair* there was loud music, exuberant dancing, psychedelic sets and nudity on stage. Subjects which in the early fifties were rarely talked about were, by the end of the sixties, shown publicly on stage.

▶ *Look Back in Anger* was revived in 1968. The play was first performed in 1956 at the Royal Court Theatre, London.

Spare time out of doors

▲ Bobby Moore, captain of the 1966 England team, triumphantly displays the World Cup after a 4–2 victory against West Germany.

'You should've seen your Dad, wandering round London in a trance singing "Land of Hope and Glory ..." all because we won a football match!'
Edward in 1966, from the Yorkshire Television series 'How We Used to Live (1954–1970)'.

More people had time and money to spend following their favourite sport, and one of the most popular sports was soccer. Television turned out to be a help rather than a rival as some people had expected. The TV coverage of matches brought soccer to a wider public. In 1958 the nation mourned when seven Manchester United players were killed in Munich when their aircraft crashed on take-off. In the 1966 World Cup Final, thousands of people shared in the triumph of the England team when they beat West Germany during extra time.

For the first time, large sums were paid in transfer fees for top players. Footballers like George Best became media stars. Older sports fans were surprised that some people seemed more interested in George's private life than in his football skills.

Cricket continued to be popular, especially the Test matches against Australia and the West Indies, but a planned tour of South Africa in 1968 was called off because South Africa objected to a black player in the English team. Sport and politics could no longer be separated, and at the 1968 Olympic Games in Mexico, black American medal-winners demonstrated for equal civil rights.

Until 1968, only amateur tennis players could compete at Wimbledon. But as more and more top players turned professional, the rules were changed to attract the best players. British supporters could only look back sadly to 1961 when Angela Mortimer beat Christine Truman in an all-English Ladies' Singles Final. From then on it seemed as if all the prizes went abroad.

Britain set some standards for the world to follow. In 1954 an English athlete, Roger Bannister, ran a mile in less than four minutes. In 1967 Sir Francis Chichester sailed round the world single-handed. He was knighted by the Queen outdoors in Greenwich. Suddenly there was a rush of interest in sailing.

For those who weren't interested in sport, there were other ways of spending the weekend. More families had cars and were able to go on picnics or visit the stately homes which were now open to the public. The Duke of Bedford added a funfair and zoo to his stately home, while thousands of West Country tourists had car stickers which said 'We have seen the lions of Longleat'.

In country areas, annual shows kept up traditions like brass bands, and in the sixties some people rediscovered morris dancing. In London, the first Notting Hill carnivals, in the fifties, drew thousands to the lively street celebrations.

Throughout the fifties and sixties there were popular fads which would suddenly arrive, seem to be everywhere for a few months, then vanish. One craze was for hula hoops – large plastic rings which spun round while you wiggled your hips. In 1959, fashionable young people were all hula hoop experts.

▲ Hula hoops were a fifties craze.

▼ In 1967 Woburn Park was used for a massive outdoor rock festival. The three biggest rock festivals were held in 1969 when the Rolling Stones played in Hyde Park, Bob Dylan played at Woodstock near New York, and on the Isle of Wight. The concerts each went on for several days.

Food and cooking

'The past winter, one of the mildest in living memory ... resulted in an exceptionally heavy spaghetti crop ... Another reason why this may be a bumper year lies in the virtual disappearance of the spaghetti weevil.'
BBC1 Panorama, April Fool's Day 1957.

In the fifties the British were unadventurous about what they ate and most knew very little about foreign food. Many viewers were taken in by Panorama's joke feature about an imaginary spaghetti harvest, and really believed that ready-made pasta grew on trees. Cooking and eating out became more interesting as larger numbers of people went abroad on holiday and came back with new ideas. Ideas were also brought to Britain by people emigrating from other countries.

▲ A faked picture of a spaghetti harvest taken from the *Panorama* April Fool programme in 1957. This was probably the last chance to fool most of the public in such a way. By the sixties people were more knowledgeable about foreign food.

▼ In 1961, people were trying new experiences. These people are smoking a hubble-bubble pipe in a Persian restaurant in London.

OLD s/d	NEW p	OLD s/d	NEW p	OLD s/d	NEW p	OLD s/d	NEW p	OLD s/d	NEW p	OLD s/d	NEW p	OLD s/d	NEW p	OLD s/d	NEW p	OLD s/d	NEW p
2/-	10	4/-	20	6/-	30	8/-	40	10/-	50	12/-	60	14/-	70	16/-	80	18/-	90
2/1	10½	4/1	20½	6/1	30½	8/1	40½	10/1	50½	12/1	60½	14/1	70½	16/1	80½	18/1	90½
2/2	11	4/2	21	6/2	31	8/2	41	10/2	51	12/2	61	14/2	71	16/2	81	18/2	91
2/3	11	4/3	21	6/3	31	8/3	41	10/3	51	12/3	61	14/3	71	16/3	81	18/3	91
2/4	11½	4/4	21½	6/4	31½	8/4	41½	10/4	51½	12/4	61½	14/4	71½	16/4	81½	18/4	91½
2/5	12	4/5	22	6/5	32	8/5	42	10/5	52	12/5	62	14/5	72	16/5	82	18/5	92
2/6	12½	4/6	22½	6/6	32½	8/6	42½	10/6	52½	12/6	62½	14/6	72½	16/6	82½	18/6	92½
2/7	13	4/7	23	6/7	33	8/7	43	10/7	53	12/7	63	14/7	73	16/7	83	18/7	93
2/8	13½	4/8	23½	6/8	33½	8/8	43½	10/8	53½	12/8	63½	14/8	73½	16/8	83½	18/8	93½
2/9	14	4/9	24	6/9	34	8/9	44	10/9	54	12/9	64	14/9	74	16/9	84	18/9	94
2/10	14	4/10	24	6/10	34	8/10	44	10/10	54	12/10	64	14/10	74	16/10	84	18/10	94
2/11	14½	4/11	24½	6/11	34½	8/11	44½	10/11	54½	12/11	64½	14/11	74½	16/11	84½	18/11	94½
3/-	15	5/-	25	7/-	35	9/-	45	11/-	55	13/-	65	15/-	75	17/-	85	19/-	95
3/1	15½	5/1	25½	7/1	35½	9/1	45½	11/1	55½	13/1	65½	15/1	75½	17/1	85½	19/1	95½
3/2	16	5/2	26	7/2	36	9/2	46	11/2	56	13/2	66	15/2	76	17/2	86	19/2	96
3/3	16	5/3	26	7/3	36	9/3	46	11/3	56	13/3	66	15/3	76	17/3	86	19/3	96
3/4	16½	5/4	26½	7/4	36½	9/4	46½	11/4	56½	13/4	66½	15/4	76½	17/4	86½	19/4	96½
3/5	17	5/5	27	7/5	37	9/5	47	11/5	57	13/5	67	15/5	77	17/5	87	19/5	97
3/6	17½	5/6	27½	7/6	37½	9/6	47½	11/6	57½	13/6	67½	15/6	77½	17/6	87½	19/6	97½
3/7	18	5/7	28	7/7	38	9/7	48	11/7	58	13/7	68	15/7	78	17/7	88	19/7	98
3/8	18½	5/8	28½	7/8	38½	9/8	48½	11/8	58½	13/8	68½	15/8	78½	17/8	88½	19/8	98½
3/9	19	5/9	29	7/9	39	9/9	49	11/9	59	13/9	69	15/9	79	17/9	89	19/9	99
3/10	19	5/10	29	7/10	39	9/10	49	11/10	59	13/10	69	15/10	79	17/10	89	19/10	99
3/11	19½	5/11	29½	7/11	39½	9/11	49½	11/11	59½	13/11	69½	15/11	79½	17/11	89½	19/11	99½

The first Chinese restaurants, which opened in the mid-fifties, offered a taste of something really different: one child thought it tasted 'like hot salad'. Until then, rice had been used mainly for milk puddings. An office worker could have a three course lunch at a Chinese restaurant for just 3/– (15p), perhaps using a luncheon voucher – part of a new scheme used by firms which didn't have canteens.

Gradually people became more ready to try something different from the plain meat and boiled vegetables they had grown up with. Italian and French cooking used a lot of new herbs and seasonings and, inevitably, there were some disasters: one woman remembers 'I used garlic in a recipe, not knowing that a clove meant one small section, not the whole head'. It wasn't until the sixties that many people tried their first kebab or curry. Asian immigrants introduced new spices to the kitchen, and Caribbeans brought over new vegetables such as sweet potatoes.

Fast food was an American idea which first came to Britain when the Wimpy bars opened in the early sixties. Frozen, tinned and dried convenience foods, which saved time and effort, were a new standby for busy people. If you wanted meat and two vegetables, you could now buy a 'TV dinner' wrapped in foil, ready to heat up and eat.

'Go to work on an egg' was a famous sixties slogan, and millions still began the day with egg and bacon. Farmers introduced intensive farming methods to increase production. Hens were packed into battery cages, and powerful chemicals were used on the land. By the end of the decade there was a growing interest in health foods, because of the influence of the 'back-to-nature' hippies. New shops opened selling unfamiliar foods like Swiss muesli and yogurt – and the clothes of the time were designed for slim figures. People went on diets to try and keep their weight down, though just over ten years earlier food had been rationed.

▲ At the end of the sixties, shoppers were being prepared for the change to decimal currency in 1971. In this supermarket, prices in shillings and pence are shown next to the decimal equivalents. Many people were worried that the change would mean higher prices.

▲ 'Cranks' opened as a health food restaurant as part of the hippies' 'back to nature' movement. In the fifties, packaged sliced white bread was very popular, but, by the end of the sixties, many people preferred to go back to wholesome home-made brown bread.

'Twist and Shout'

'I remember listening to *She Loves You* at a school dance, and having to put my hands over my ears because of the screaming. A teacher told me later that I'd been screaming too!'
Sue, aged 11 in 1963

The pop music revolution began in 1955. The pounding beat of Bill Haley's *Rock Around the Clock* burst into the charts and was enthusiastically welcomed by teenagers who recognised that at last here was their own music, and something completely different from old-fashioned 'crooners' their parents enjoyed. The new sound was loud, fast and young, and the Top Ten would never be the same again. Adults were amazed to hear about teenagers ripping up cinema seats so they could rock 'n' roll in the aisles.

The rock 'n' roll sound came from the USA and, until the early sixties, the music charts were dominated by American singers. Elvis Presley had fifteen number one records from 1957–65, hits like *Jailhouse Rock* and *Blue Suede Shoes*. In his early years, his dancing was thought too rude to be shown on TV so he was always filmed above the waist.

Britain's answer to Elvis was Cliff Richard, with one big difference – mums liked Cliff. Other British stars included cheerful Tommy Steele and the folksy skiffle groups. They didn't quite match the excitement of wild American singers like Jerry Lee Lewis and Little Richard. Romantic soul ballads were also in the charts, and a popular mixture of beat and sentiment lasted through the sixties.

▶ Most record shops had booths where customers could listen to records before buying them. The heavy reel-to-reel tape recorders of the fifties were quickly outsold by cassette recorders in the sixties.

▲ The Beatles – Paul, George, Ringo and John – had a string of international hit records and films. In 1965 they were awarded the MBE.

▲ Jimi Hendrix was a singer and guitarist who became famous in the sixties for the extraordinary sound he produced from his guitar in songs like *Purple Haze* and *Electric Ladyland*. At the end of the decade he died from a drug overdose.

▶ After the success of the Beatles, many other Liverpool musicians and poets became famous, including Cilla Black who recorded the Top Ten hit, *Step Inside Love*.

In 1962 the Beatles appeared on the pop scene and by 1963 they had rocketed to international fame with songs like *Please Please Me*. Pop music was the new boom industry. No one could have predicted the passionate devotion of thousands of fans to their pop idols, or the way they would follow any fashion set by the musicians, from haircuts to transcendental meditation.

From the start, rock music had been rebellious, but in the sixties one issue caused a major clash between the pop world and the Establishment – drug taking. Many groups, including the Beatles, the Who and the Rolling Stones were reported to experiment with dangerous mind-bending drugs. But their fans were mainly concerned with the music.

In the charts were cheerful songs by groups like the Supremes, while other groups who rarely entered the singles charts had huge followings at massively attended open-air pop festivals. These groups included Pink Floyd, Procul Harum and Soft Machine in Britain and the Grateful Dead, Velvet Underground, Jimi Hendrix and the Doors in the USA.

In 1965 Bob Dylan sang *The times they are a'changing* and the Who about *My Generation*. Yet many of these rebellious sixties singers were still making hits two decades later.

Fifties fashion, sixties style

'I was always getting my stiletto heels stuck between paving slabs, and going home on the bus with only one shoe on'
Sue, aged 12 in 1964

In the fifties many men began to be more fashion-conscious, particularly a group known as the Teddy Boys. They looked down on 'squares' – men who still dressed like their fathers and had short-back-and-sides hair cuts. The Teddy Boy uniform was long draped jackets, drainpipe trousers, shoe-string ties and 'beetle-crusher' shoes with thick soles. You could always recognise a Teddy Boy by his hairstyle – greased back into a 'DA' with the back flipped up like a duck's tail, quiffs stuck together with Brylcream, and Elvis Presley side-boards. Most people's overwhelming impression of the Teds is that they were always combing their hair.

The 'with-it' shape for women kept changing, from full gathered dirndl skirts supported by stiff frou-frou petticoats, to pencil-slim skirts and black 'sloppy Joe' sweaters – often borrowed from a boyfriend. Dresses had waistlines on the hips or none at all, or strapless bodices with little jackets called 'boleros'.

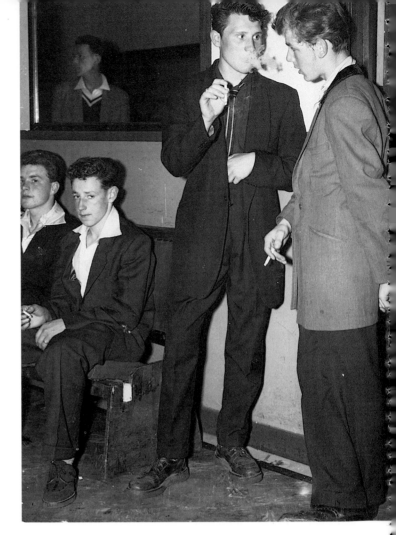

▲ Fifties Teddy boys dressed up for the evening. A full Teddy boy outfit could cost as much as two months wages.

▼ A 1966 wedding. While the bride wears a traditional dress, her groom is wearing a 'mod' outfit. Women guests wear the latest fashions – trouser suits, miniskirts and string dresses.

Under their dresses women wore stockings (or nylons as they were known), which were held up by elastic roll-on girdles and suspender belts. Shoes ranged from absolutely flat ballerina styles to pointed toes and narrow high stiletto heels which ruined floors.

Fifties women wore their hair backcombed into a stiff shape called a 'beehive' and lacquered into place, or pinned back in a complicated French pleat. Some women copied the actress Audrey Hepburn and cut their hair into short elfin wisps. One of the simplest styles was a ponytail which in winter could be pulled through a hole at the top of a woolly hat.

Long-haired arty intellectuals were nicknamed 'beatniks'. They were recognisable by their duffel coats, draped with long scarves often with a CND badge pinned on to show they were against the nuclear bomb. It was a fashion worn both by boys and girls to show they had ideals in common.

Tights were a liberating sixties invention after draughty stockings and suspenders. Now there was less reason for girls to hide the tops of their legs and hemlines rose. The mini-skirt caught on rapidly; tiny micro-mini skirts were called pelmets and barely covered a girl's bottom. A whole new look appeared with the mini-skirt. Girls strode round in tall plastic boots or clumpy shoes, and sometimes wore huge-brimmed floppy hats from the 'Biba' boutique.

▲ The winner of a 1966 teenage hairstyle competition. Her hair is backcombed into a 'bouffant' style and held in place with laquer.

▲ In 1961, people from all over the world joined in a 'ban the bomb' protest march. Typical student protesters wore polo neck jumpers and narrow trews, with duffel coats and flat shoes.

◄ Miniskirts became shorter and shorter.

31

Mods, rockers and flower children

> 'I remember an almost space-age geometric look … I longed for dead straight glossy hair and skinny legs.'
> *Jenny, aged 18 in 1966*

Sixties designers experimented with zany new materials for clothes: throwaway paper dresses had a brief surge of popularity, also chain-mail, PVC and plastic, but no one took them seriously. Clothes weren't designed to last, just to be fun.

Geometric haircuts were all the rage, cut in straight lines with triangular fringes over one eye. All girls wanted to have dead straight hair: one woman remembers ironing her hair between sheets of brown paper. By the end of the decade, 'Afro' styles were in fashion and the same girls were trying to frizz their hair. Eyes were heavily made-up with false eyelashes and lots of mascara, and some girls used eyebrow pencils to paint on fake freckles.

▲ By the end of the sixties, girls hunted for fashionable clothes in their grannies' attics or the Oxfam shop. Men wore patchwork trousers, beads and Indian scarves, and let their hair grow long and bushy.

While girls in the fifties had spent a lot of time trying to look older, sixties women tried to look childlike. The top model of the sixties was Twiggy. Slim, young and working class, she was more photographed than royalty.

Teenage culture had its own groups. Mods were successors to the Teds. They wore smart clothes, and travelled around on scooters covered with as many badges, lamps and pennants as they could squash on. Rockers rode heavy motorbikes and dressed in menacing black leather. On Bank Holidays, thousands of Mods and Rockers made for seaside resorts. The resulting fights were news headlines..

In the late sixties, 'Skinheads' ganged together. Their uniform was denim trousers and braces, with huge 'bovver' boots, and their trademark of hair shaved to the scalp. Many people saw 'dreadlocks' for the first time when the Caribbean cult of Rastafarianism spread to Britain in the late sixties. Followers dressed in the bright colours of the Ethiopian flag and did not cut their hair.

▲ The early sixties 'dolly bird' look was long straight hair and a pale face. No red-haired girl would ever have worn a plum-coloured dress before this period.

▲ Twiggy, a model known as 'the face of the sixties'.

'Hippies' or 'Flower children' were influenced by what they saw as the mystic East. They believed in peace, love and an alternative life-style to previous generations. They rejected 'bread heads' – anyone who they felt was more interested in money than in 'finding themselves'. Hippies wore kaftans, frayed at the edges and decorated with beads, bells and flowers. Many took 'mind expanding' drugs.

Throughout the sixties, London was the fashion centre of the world. Tourists flocked to the boutiques of Carnaby Street and the King's Road to buy clothes – from mini skirts to maxi coats so long they caught in escalators, bright military uniforms or romantic Laura Ashley cotton prints. For the first time, it became acceptable for women to wear trouser suits. Even so, in 1970 women in the accounts department of Yorkshire Television were sent home for wearing trousers!

◀ In the mid-sixties, five young typists offered to work extra hours for no money, to help Britain's struggling economy. This turned into the 'I'm Backing Britain' campaign, and for a while there was a fashion for wearing clothes covered in Union Jacks.

▲ Mary Quant was a top designer who brought British fashion to the attention of the world. She was part of an small group who influenced taste and style in the sixties.

◀ Carnaby Street was one of the brightest parts of 'swinging London'. It was lined with boutiques selling the most up-to-date fashions.

In the news

'All the freedom fighters in Hungary were crying out for someone to help them when the Russians moved in. We should have gone to their aid, if we hadn't been so busy over Suez.'

Michael, from the Yorkshire Television series 'How We Used to Live (1954–1970)'

During the same weeks as the Suez Crisis, young Hungarians were struggling for freedom from Russian dominance. They were crushed as Russian tanks rolled into the streets of Budapest. A similar uprising against Soviet authority in Czechoslovakia in 1968 was also ruthlessly suppressed.

The Suez Canal is a vital stretch of international waterway which runs through Egypt, linking the Red Sea and the Mediterranean. In the early fifties it was under the control of the British and the French, but in 1956 the ruler of Egypt, Colonel Nasser, seized the Canal. Britain and France were afraid that Nasser would close the Canal and cut off their oil supplies from the Middle East. They secretly prepared for war, with Israel as an ally. Israel sent troops to the Suez Canal and Britain followed, ordered by the Prime Minister, Anthony Eden. This was condemned at home and in America. Eventually they were forced to withdraw. It was no longer possible to control Egypt by force from London. Britain had to get used to being a second-class power dependent on help from her allies.

Suspicion between the two new super powers of the USA and the Soviet Union grew worse. With the development of nuclear weapons and space technology on both sides, each suspected the other of hostile intentions in an atmosphere that became known as the Cold War. Each side tried to learn the other's military secrets.

The Russians were embarrassed by the steady stream of people, including top scientists, who were leaving Communist countries and defecting to the West. The border between east and west Berlin was a major escape route and, in 1961, this border was sealed. Anyone trying to escape across it would be shot by border guards.

Spies were frequently in the news throughout the fifties and sixties. Some, like Burgess and Maclean, escaped to Russia before they could be arrested; their partner, Kim Philby wasn't discovered until 1963. Spies were sometimes exchanged; the Krogers who had been arrested in 1961, were released in 1969 and sent to Moscow in exchange for Gerald Brooke who had been arrested for anti-Soviet activities in Moscow in 1965.

A major scandal in 1963 affected the British Government. John Profumo, Secretary of State for War, was accused of seeing a call-girl, Christine Keeler, who was also involved with a Russian naval captain. It was unlikely that Britain's defence secrets were given away, but the Press made headlines of all the sordid details and caused the Prime Minister, Harold Macmillan, great embarrassment.

South Africa's ruling minority of white people had no plans to share the country's government or the best jobs, education and home life, with black people. When Britain refused to support this policy of apartheid, South Africa left the Commonwealth. The rest of the world was shocked by the brutality of the pass laws which severely restricted the rights and movements of black people in South Africa. In Sharpeville in 1960, a group of black people were massacred for protesting against these laws.

John F. Kennedy was elected as President of the United States of America in 1960. He was handsome, young and charming, and for many Americans he represented the new mood of prosperity and confidence. He promised to 'get America moving again'. One of his greatest challenges was the Cuban crisis. The Russians had been installing nuclear weapons on Cuba, an island off the coast of America. Kennedy sent a naval blockade until the Russians withdrew. Kennedy supported civil rights, and was a friend of Martin Luther King. The world was shocked when Kennedy was assassinated in 1963.

In the news

'I have a dream that my four little children will one day live in a nation where they will not be judged by the colour of their skin, but by the content of their character.'
Martin Luther King addressing a civil rights meeting in 1963.

The shadow of the Vietnam war hung over the Sixties. Russia intervened in the civil war between North and South Vietnam, to help the Communist North. There were fears that China would also join in. The USA sent troops in to South Vietnam against what they saw as Communist aggression. The war became one of indiscriminate destruction and civilians suffered terrible atrocities. In America, many people reacted by staging protests, and many young people left the country to avoid being drafted into the army. In the seventies, America was finally forced to withdraw from Vietnam.

Although in the fifties the American government banned racial discrimination, some states broke the law and continued to separate black and white people on buses, in schools, in cinemas and other public places. Black people found a leader in Martin Luther King who led many peaceful demonstrations for civil rights. His courage and leadership helped to unite black Americans and bring the issue of civil rights to public attention. Tragically, he was assassinated in 1968.

The fragile peace that existed in Northern Ireland between Catholics and Protestants was broken in 1969, mainly because of fears about growing unemployment. The IRA became more active, particularly after the Government banned marches. After several violent incidents the Government sent over troops to try to keep the peace. Some people tried to resolve the conflict including Bernadette Devlin, who was a 23 year old student when she was elected to Parliament to represent the Catholic minority.

In 1953 the Soviet Union had successfully tested a nuclear hydrogen bomb. Russia and America had weapons of equal destructive power. The first British H-bomb was exploded in 1957 at Christmas Island in the Pacific. Testers often failed to guard against the full effects of radiation, as one man remembers: 'My cousin was there. They were told to turn their backs and shade their eyes.' Many people were worried as nuclear testing was stepped up. They were afraid of radioactive fall-out, and chemicals in their milk. In 1958 the Campaign for Nuclear Disarmament was founded to 'Ban the Bomb'. Every Easter, protesters marched from London to the nuclear base at Aldermaston. The marches grew rapidly in size during the late fifties and early sixties.

The Vietnam war triggered student protest against all war. Many students supported the Chinese communist leader Chairman Mao, and rejected capitalism. They rebelled against the older generation who, they felt, had made a mess of things. Rioting became violent in Paris and spread to the USA where police fought with demonstrating students. In Britain, the London School of Economics had the most radical students, although there were demonstrations and sit-ins held all over the country.

In the sixties, China was one of the major world powers, and had the H-bomb. It was ruled by Mao Tse-tung, whom some people consider to be one of the most influential leaders this century. He revolutionised Chinese communism, believing in the power of the peasants. One of his ideas was to set up farming communes where city workers could work side by side with peasants. Millions of Chinese carried Mao's thoughts written in his 'Little Red Book'. China closed itself off from the rest of the world during the sixties, and people were shocked by the reports of fighting led by violent bands of students called the Red Guards.

▲ Rescue workers at the Aberfan disaster on 22nd October 1966.

Caring

'It had rained non-stop all the autumn term in Cardiff. A lecturer came in looking stricken and asked for some moments of silence. The rugby team went out to Aberfan and dug all night. They returned completely black except for tear stains.'
Jenny, a college student aged 20 in 1966

One morning in 1966, as children in a South Wales mining village settled down to school, a landslide moved a vast tip of coal waste down the hill. The whole school was buried in a smothering mass, and 116 children and 28 adults were killed. The nation watched the rescue attempts on television, sick with sympathy for the grieving parents whose children's bodies were being dug out of the wrecked classrooms. This horrific disaster could have been prevented, and many people felt that industrial progress was being made without enough thought for human life.

Six months later a huge oil tanker, called the 'Torrey Canyon', was wrecked off the coast of Cornwall. Giant oil slicks formed on the surface of the sea, and crude oil spread on the beaches along the south coast. Thousands of dead sea birds and fish were washed up every day. Concerned people tried to help but there was little they could do, and eventually the Navy had to bomb the tanker.

By the end of the sixties people had become much more aware of pollution of the environment and the danger to wildlife, and were determined to change things. In 1963 a book by Rachel Carson, *Silent Spring*, warned of a planet poisoned by chemical pollution. Many people began to recognise that prosperity now might be storing up horrors for the future.

◄ The wreck of the oil tanker, the 'Torrey Canyon', lying off the coast of Cornwall in March 1967.

Television brought home the contrast between the wealth in Britain, and the starvation and suffering in some developing countries. The fifties and sixties showed a huge increase in the work of aid organisations such as Oxfam. Help was given to refugees and victims of civil war, and research was carried out into the causes of hunger, poverty and disease. As the result of a newspaper article, Amnesty International was set up to work for the release of people imprisoned because of their religious or political beliefs.

In Britain, there were still many people caught in the 'poverty trap' without enough money to live on. A new charity, Shelter, was founded to put pressure on the government to provide housing for everyone, and to set up projects such as making derelict houses fit to live in.

The Church showed a new image, to keep up with the changes in society. The New English Bible was published in 1961. It was written in modern English to make it easier to understand and was an immediate bestseller. A year later, in Coventry, a new modern cathedral was opened.

▲ Children from a Hampshire school collecting gifts to raise money for Oxfam. Television pictures of the victims of civil war in Biafra captured the sympathy of viewers.

Work which had been done by church volunteers was now done by professional social workers. But many people suffered from the pace of change and the Samaritans were started in the sixties to help desperate and lonely people. Community care groups were formed, often in schools where pupils would do jobs such as weeding a pensioner's garden.

◄ One week's political activities in 1969, listed in the London magazine 'Time Out'.

▼ Cathy Come Home was a drama documentary about a homeless family, which was first shown on television in 1966. It had a huge impact on viewers and helped to make people far more aware of the other side of the prosperous sixties.

Science and invention

'Science was making our world seem smaller but somehow more complex.'
Marty, a teacher aged 25 in 1963

In the fifties and sixties many people thought that science would provide the answer to the world's problems. The government was keen to promote research and during this period there were a variety of new discoveries and inventions. Some were on a massive scale, like the world's first nuclear power station at Calder Hall, or the enormous Jodrell Bank radio telescope tilted towards the stars.

Other discoveries were invisible to the naked eye. In Cambridge, scientists discovered DNA, the molecule which makes up genes and decides the nature of every living thing from an elephant to a virus. The study of DNA became the basis of research into cancer and other diseases.

In the mid-fifties doctors could at last vaccinate against the crippling disease of polio, and in 1963, a vaccine against measles was perfected. Surgery became news in 1967 when Dr Christian Barnard performed the first heart transplant.

The contraceptive pill was widely available from 1961, and gave women more control over whether or not to have children. It was opposed by some people and Roman Catholics were forbidden to use it.

Medical science received a severe shock when it was found that a new drug, Thalidomide, given to some pregnant mothers, affected the development of unborn babies. Tragically they were born with deformed limbs.

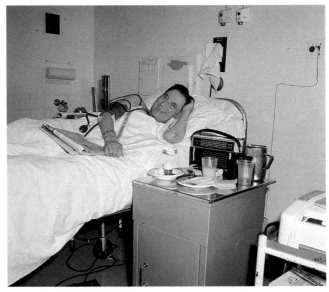

▲ Medical technology continued to improve in 1967. This patient was the first person to have a successful heart transplant operation.

▲ The Queen opened Calder Hall nuclear power station in 1956. Most people were enthusiastic about nuclear power, and the new jobs it created. Later, some began to have doubts about its safety.

◄ The first computers took up several rooms, and the floors had to be strengthened to take their weight. Computers did not become desk-sized until the late sixties.

There were disappointments in the aircraft industry, too. A new jet airliner, Comet, seemed destined for a successful future, but three crashes in a year were caused by metal fatigue. By the late sixties, engineers in Britain and France were jointly researching and building Concorde, the world's first supersonic jet to carry passengers.

With more people travelling abroad there was a demand for new forms of transport. In 1959, the hovercraft was revealed to the public. At first it was used only for short journeys but by 1968 there were regular services across the Channel every day.

Telephoning long distance was speeded up with STD direct dialling, which meant that calls no longer had to be connected by the operator.

In the mid-sixties a reserve of energy was discovered in the North Sea. Many homes were connected to North Sea gas, and Britain became an oil-producing country.

Smaller discoveries also made a difference to everyday life. Banks introduced cash dispenser machines in 1967, and the first ring-pull cans and fibre-tip pens were on sale in the sixties.

▲ Concorde 002 on its maiden flight in 1967. Many people admired its design, but others, who lived under the aircraft's flight-path, didn't like the bang when it broke the sound barrier.

▲ In 1965, the first cheap 'instant print' polaroid cameras became widely available.

▲ Visitors to a Moscow exhibition in 1958, looking at a model of Sputnik III.

▲ Ham, the American chimpanzee astronaut, successfully returned to earth in 1967 after his space journey.

▲ A photograph taken on the moon shows Buzz Aldrin after the first successful landing.

Man on the moon

'Elderly patients I nursed couldn't believe that a man was on the moon. They had seen the first motor cars.'
Tessa, a nurse aged 23 in 1969

In 1957 the first satellite, a Russian Sputnik, was launched into orbit – the space race had started. Satellites were sent into space carrying scientific equipment to collect information and send it back. The scientists began to experiment with the possibility that living creatures could survive in space, and dogs, monkeys and other animals were sent up.

The first man to go into space was a Russian, Yuri Gagarin, in 1961. Two years later, Valentina Tereshkova proved that women could also be cosmonauts. In 1965, Alexei Leonov took a walk in space, which meant that repairs and tests could be made from outside the craft.

The Americans were determined to catch up. Their Apollo space programme was launched with the aim of getting men on the moon. America quickly followed the Soviet Union by sending up a manned space craft in 1962.

In July 1969, the Apollo 11 rocket was launched from Cape Kennedy. It contained astronauts Collins, Aldrin and Armstrong on a journey to the moon. After four days, the lunar module was detached from the main spacecraft for the moon landing, with Aldrin and Armstrong aboard. Collins, in the command-service module, stayed in orbit round the moon while his two colleagues made a soft landing on the rocky dusty surface.

Neil Armstrong was the first man to set foot on the moon. His words were: 'I am going to step off the module now. That is one small step for man, one giant leap for mankind.' Over 373 000 kms away, across the world 600 million people watched him on television.

King, Martin Luther

Campaigner for black civil rights in the USA. He was a Baptist minister who led peaceful protest marches and demonstrations. He was assassinated in 1968.

Krushchev, Nikita

Russian leader from 1953, after Stalin's death. He broke off relations with China, and believed in peaceful co-existence with the West, although he often pretended to be enraged at important meetings—at the United Nations, he once took off his shoes and thumped them on the table. He said, 'Rock and roll music and outlandish fashions ... can only appeal to those who are not quite right in the head.' He was dismissed in 1964.

Macmillan, Harold

Conservative Prime Minister 1957–1963. He was nicknamed 'Supermac' during the years of Britain's spending boom. He introduced Premium Bonds, and encouraged the independence of African states.

▲ Pop brought its own new celebrities. Jimmy Savile was a disc jockey from a Northern working class background. He helped the BBC to have a younger image.

Nureyev, Rudolf

Ballet dancer. Born on a train in Siberia, he defected to the West in 1961 while on tour with the Kirov Ballet in Paris. His dancing, especially with Margot Fonteyn, added new excitement to ballet.

Olivier, Laurence

Actor, best known for his performances in Shakespeare and elegant comedy roles. In 1958 he played a broken-down music hall artist in *The Entertainer*, a play by 'angry young man' John Osborne, as a sign that he welcomed new writing.

Picasso, Pablo

In the early years of the century, his paintings broke all art traditions. By the fifties and sixties they began to fetch enormously high prices.

Quant, Mary

British fashion designer who began with a boutique, 'Bazaar' in Chelsea. Her success made London the fashion centre of the world in the sixties. Her styles suggested youth and freedom, and were copied by chain stores.

Russell, Bertrand

Socialist philosopher. He was 85 when he founded and became president of CND in Britain. In 1961 he spent a week in prison for demonstrating against the Polaris nuclear submarine base.

Warhol, Andy

American artist, important in the Pop Art movement. Famous for paintings of tins of soup and of Marilyn Monroe. Many of his works were silk screen prints, and were often seen on posters.

Wilson, Harold

Labour Prime Minister 1964–1970. He felt that the future depended on science and technology, when Britain's economic boom was fading. He introduced comprehensive schools and founded the Open University, but also had to face industrial disputes and troubles in Northern Ireland.

▲ Marilyn Monroe was an American film star and sex symbol in the fifties. Her films include *Some Like It Hot* and *The Seven Year Itch*.

Some important events 1954–1970

1954

Food rationing ended in Britain.
USA tested the H-bomb.
Algerians used terrorism to fight for independence from France.
Roger Bannister became the first person to run a mile in less than four minutes.

1955

Conservatives won the General Election,
Anthony Eden became Prime Minister.
Moves to abolish hanging after Ruth Ellis executed for killing her lover.
Films – *Rock Around the Clock* and *Rebel Without A Cause* had a large teenage following.
Introduction of the Duke of Edinburgh's Award scheme.
Fighting on Cyprus between Greek and Turkish Cypriots.
Craze for reporting sights of flying saucers.

1956

Calder Hall started supplying nuclear power.
Suez crisis – Britain sent troops to Egypt but was forced to withdraw them.
Hungarian uprising against rule from Moscow.
Look Back In Anger produced at the Royal Court Theatre.

1957

France, Belgium, West Germany, Luxembourg, Holland and Italy set up the Common Market.
Ghana became an independent African state.
Britain has the H-bomb.
Eden resigned. Harold Macmillan took over as Prime Minister.
The Russians launched Sputniks I and II.
ERNIE drew first Premium Bond prizes.

▶ Thousands of people queued to see the funeral of Sir Winston Churchill in 1965.

1958

Notting Hill race riots.
Munich air disaster – seven Manchester United players killed.
Early tower blocks built.
CND launched. First march to Aldermaston.
Hula-hoop craze peaks.

1959

Conservatives again won the General Election.
Left-wing rebel Fidel Castro took power in Cuba.
First cross-channel hovercraft test at Cowes.

1960

Disarmament talks took place in Geneva.
American spy, Gary Powers, had his plane shot down while he was spying over Russia. This caused embarrassment to the Americans during the disarmament talks.
John F. Kennedy elected President of the USA.
The Queen launched the first British nuclear submarine.
The farthing went out of circulation.

1961

The border between East and West Berlin was sealed by the Berlin Wall.
Trial in Jerusalem of the Nazi war criminal Adolf Eichmann. He was later hanged.
Workers strike for tea breaks.
Yuri Gagarin became the first man to go into space.
The book, *Lady Chatterley's Lover*, on trial for obscenity.

1962

The Cuba crisis. Soviet nuclear missiles were installed on the island, then removed after President Kennedy set up a naval blockade. Widespread fear of nuclear war.
The United Nations Assembly demanded an end to nuclear testing.
Algeria became independent from France.
Craze for dancing the Twist.

1963

'The Great Train Robbery'. An armed gang stole £2½ million from a mail train.
President Kennedy assassinated.
Coldest winter for years – River Thames freezes.
Newsom report recommended raising the school leaving age from 15 to 16.

1964

Labour won the General Election, Harold Wilson became Prime Minister.
US troops intervened in Vietnam war.
Mods and Rockers fought on Brighton beach.
Olympic Games held in Tokyo.
A new newspaper, the *Sun*, went on sale.
Top of the Pops first broadcast.
The Post Office tower was opened.

1965

Winston Churchill died.
Capital punishment was abolished.
War between India and Pakistan.
New aviary at London Zoo, designed by Lord Snowdon.
The Rent Act gave greater security to tenants.

1966

The Labour Party increased its majority at the General Election.
Aberfan slag-heap disaster.
The Vietnam war escalated.
The World Cup was stolen. It was later found in a London garden.
England beat West Germany in the World Cup final.
The government declared a state of emergency during the seamen's strike to safeguard food supplies.
The 'Moors murderers', Ian Brady and Myra Hindley, were convicted for torturing and killing children. This led to a campaign to bring back hanging.

1967

'I'm Backing Britain' campaign.
The Six Day War – Israel fought against Egypt, Syria and Jordan.
Donald Campbell dies in 'Bluebird' while attempting the world speed record on Coniston Water.
The 'Torrey Canyon' ran aground off Land's End.
Civil war in Nigeria.
First programmes shown in colour on television.

▲ The Queen opens the Victoria Line on the London Underground in 1968.

1968

Three people killed when part of the Ronan Point tower block collapsed after an explosion.
Widespread student unrest and riots.
Demonstration against the Vietnam war held outside the American embassy.
Dr Martin Luther King assassinated.
Russian army goes into Czechoslovakia.
Olympic Games held in Mexico City.
A new section of the London Underground, the Victoria Line, was opened.
First issue of 5p and 10p decimal coins.

1969

Apollo 11 landed on the moon. Neil Armstrong and Buzz Aldrin were the first people to walk on the moon.
Three major pop festivals held; Woodstock, the Isle of Wight, and the Rolling Stones in Hyde Park.
British troops go into Northern Ireland following clashes between Catholics and Protestants.
Investiture of the Prince of Wales.
Widespread strikes against government legislation.
Student sit-in at the London School of Economics.

1970

The Conservatives won the General Election, Edward Heath became Prime Minister.
Young people are allowed to vote at 18.
Divorce laws made easier – 'Gingerbread' group formed to help one-parent families.
Jumbo Jets introduced.

Index

This index will help you to find some of the important things in *How We Used to Live*. The page numbers shown in **dark letters** refer to illustrations. The dates, *in italics*, show you where to look in the 'Important Events' section on pages 46–47.